BABY NAME :

D1373294

Happy
Easter

Thank you for your Purchase!
We hope that you like this Book!

Please fell free to share what you like or dislike
about it by submitting a **Review**.
This Will help as improve it and serve you better.
Without Your Voice We Don't Exist!

Thank you so mush for your time and support!

Copyright © 2022 Mr. Alae
All Rights Reserved